EASY PLUM COOKBOOK

A PLUM BOOK FILLED WITH 50 DELICIOUS PLUM RECIPES

By
BookSumo Press
Copyright © by Saxonberg Associates
All rights reserved

Published by
BookSumo Press, a DBA of Saxonberg Associates
http://www.booksumo.com/

Join the BookSumo Private Reader's Club and get a massive collection of 6 cookbooks!

The first set of cookbook is for the lovers of easy cooking.

You will get the "Easy Specialty Cookbook Box Set" for FREE!

This box set includes the following cookbooks:

1. Easy Sushi Cookbook
2. Easy Dump Dinner Cookbook
3. Easy Beans Cookbook

AND for the ethnic and cultural food lovers you will also get the "Easy Cultural Cookbook Box Set" for FREE as well!

This box set includes the following cookbooks:

1. A Kitchen in Morocco
2. Easy Samosas & Pot Pie Recipes
3. The Biryani Bash

Join the group of private readers, and enjoy these cookbooks. This collection is only available for private readers and it's over 400 pages when printed! Plus you will receive fun updates, and musings about food and cooking.

6 Cookbooks. 400+ pages of recipes. Everything delicious and easy.

To get these 6 free books just stay to the end of this cookbook and follow the directions at the back!

ABOUT THE AUTHOR.

BookSumo Press is a publisher of unique, easy, and healthy cookbooks.

Our cookbooks span all topics and all subjects. If you want a deep dive into the possibilities of cooking with any type of ingredient. Then BookSumo Press is your go to place for robust yet simple and delicious cookbooks and recipes. Whether you are looking for great tasting pressure cooker recipes or authentic ethic and cultural food. BookSumo Press has a delicious and easy cookbook for you.

With simple ingredients, and even simpler step-by-step instructions BookSumo cookbooks get everyone in the kitchen chefing delicious meals.

BookSumo is an independent publisher of books operating in the beautiful Garden State (NJ) and our team of chefs and kitchen experts are here to teach, eat, and be merry!

INTRODUCTION

Welcome to *The Effortless Chef Series*! Thank you for taking the time to purchase this cookbook.

Come take a journey into the delights of easy cooking. The point of this cookbook and all BookSumo Press cookbooks is to exemplify the effortless nature of cooking simply.

In this book we focus on Plum. You will find that even though the recipes are simple, the taste of the dishes are quite amazing.

So will you take an adventure in simple cooking? If the answer is yes please consult the table of contents to find the dishes you are most interested in.

Once you are ready, jump right in and start cooking.

— BookSumo Press

Table of Contents

Join the BookSumo Private Reader's Club and get a massive collection of 6 cookbooks! 2

About the Author 6

Introduction 7

Table of Contents 8

Any Issues? Contact Us 13

Legal Notes 14

Common Abbreviations 15

Chapter 1: Easy Plum Recipes 16

    Homemade Asian Plum Sauce 16

    Countryside Plum Crisp 18

    Potato and Plum Dumplings 21

    Easy Homemade Plum Cake 24

Cinnamon Clove and Plum Bread 27

German Plum Cake 30

(Kuchen) 30

A Very Light Flan 33

Plum Jelly 101 36

How to Make Tapioca Pudding 39

Rustic Pie 42

Moist Homemade Plum Lemon Cake 46

Traditional French Dessert 49

Jalapeno Plum Chipotle Sauce 52

Persian Inspired Cardamom and Plum Jam 56

New Age Plum Cake 59

Agave Butter 62

Fruity Plum Rolls German Style 65

Plum Poblano Salsa 68

Plum No Sugar Butter 70

Asian Inspired Chicken 72

Autumnal Warm Baked Plums 74

Gourmet Chicken 77

Pretty Cake 80

Thursday's Dinner Plum Chicken With Rice 83

Mediterrean Plum Salad 86

Lunch Box Chicken 89

Artisanal Plum Roasted Chicken 92

Cobbler French Style 94

Healthy Fruit Medley Crumble 97

Best Breakfast Muffins 100

Richly Spiced Raisin and Plum Chutney 103

3-Ingredient Jam 106

Tempting Plums 108

I ♥ Plum Jam 110

Shining ★ Muffins 113

Latin Orange Buttery Flan 116

Friday Night Plum Steak 119

Yummy Candies 122

Zesty Sorbet With Plums and Orange 124

Miami Spritzers 126

Enticing Plums 129

Comforting Beef Dinner 132

Thai Style Sauce 135

Swiss Style Cake 138

Lemon Cardamom and Plum Sauce 142

Fresh Salad Armenian Style 145

Salmon Asian Style 148

Fruit & Sushi Rice Spring Rolls 150

Jerk Stir-Fry 153

(Caribbean) 153

Tofu Stir Fry 156

THANKS FOR READING! JOIN THE CLUB AND KEEP ON COOKING WITH 6 MORE COOKBOOKS 159

Come On 161

Let's Be Friends :)..161

Any Issues? Contact Us

If you find that something important to you is missing from this book please contact us at info@booksumo.com.

We will take your concerns into consideration when the 2nd edition of this book is published. And we will keep you updated!

— BookSumo Press

LEGAL NOTES

ALL RIGHTS RESERVED. NO PART OF THIS BOOK MAY BE REPRODUCED OR TRANSMITTED IN ANY FORM OR BY ANY MEANS. PHOTOCOPYING, POSTING ONLINE, AND / OR DIGITAL COPYING IS STRICTLY PROHIBITED UNLESS WRITTEN PERMISSION IS GRANTED BY THE BOOK'S PUBLISHING COMPANY. LIMITED USE OF THE BOOK'S TEXT IS PERMITTED FOR USE IN REVIEWS WRITTEN FOR THE PUBLIC.

Common Abbreviations

cup(s)	C.
tablespoon	tbsp
teaspoon	tsp
ounce	oz.
pound	lb

*All units used are standard American measurements

Chapter 1: Easy Plum Recipes

Homemade Asian Plum Sauce

Ingredients

- 3/4 (16 oz.) jar plum jam
- 2 tbsp vinegar
- 1 tbsp brown sugar
- 1 tbsp dried minced onion
- 1 tsp crushed red pepper flakes
- 1 clove garlic, minced
- 1/2 tsp ground ginger

Directions

- In a pan, mix together the jam, vinegar, brown sugar, dried onion, red pepper, garlic and ginger on medium heat and bring to a boil, stirring continuously.
- Remove from the heat.

Amount per serving (10 total)

Timing Information:

Preparation	5 m
Cooking	15 m
Total Time	20 m

Nutritional Information:

Calories	102 kcal
Fat	0.1 g
Carbohydrates	25.1g
Protein	0.2 g
Cholesterol	0 mg
Sodium	11 mg

* Percent Daily Values are based on a 2,000 calorie diet.

Countryside Plum Crisp

Ingredients

- 12 plums, pitted and chopped
- 1 C. white sugar, divided
- 1 C. sifted all-purpose flour
- 1 1/2 tsp baking powder
- 1 tsp salt
- 1 beaten egg
- 1/2 C. melted butter

Directions

- Set your oven to 350 degrees F before doing anything else and grease an 8x8-inch baking dish.
- In the bottom of the prepared baking dish, arrange the chopped plums and sprinkle with 1/4 C. of the sugar.
- In a bowl, mix together 3/4 C. of the white sugar, flour, baking powder and salt.
- Add the beaten egg and mix till combined.

- Place the flour mixture over the plums evenly and drizzle with the melted butter.
- Cook in the oven for about 40 minutes.

Amount per serving (6 total)

Timing Information:

Preparation	15 m
Cooking	40 m
Total Time	55 m

Nutritional Information:

Calories	414 kcal
Fat	16.7 g
Carbohydrates	64.7g
Protein	4.3 g
Cholesterol	72 mg
Sodium	631 mg

* Percent Daily Values are based on a 2,000 calorie diet.

Potato and Plum Dumplings

Ingredients

- 3 tbsp butter
- 1 C. dry bread crumbs
- 4 large russet potatoes, peeled
- 1 tbsp butter
- 2 C. all-purpose flour
- 1 egg
- 1 pinch salt
- 16 Italian prune plums, pitted and left whole
- 16 tsp white sugar, divided

Directions

- In a skillet, melt 3 tbsp of the butter on medium-low heat and stir fry the bread crumbs for about 2 minutes.
- Remove from the heat and keep aside.
- In a pan of water, add the potatoes on medium heat and boil for about 20-30 minutes.
- Drain the potatoes and keep aside to cool for several minutes.

- Through a potato ricer, squeeze the potatoes into a bowl.
- Add 1 tbsp of the butter into the potatoes and let it melt.
- Add the flour and mix till well combined.
- Add the egg and salt and mix well.
- Place the potato mixture onto a generously floured surface and knead for about 10 minutes.
- Divide the dough into quarters and subdivide each quarter into fourths to make 16 portions.
- Make a ball from each portion and roll the ball out on a floured surface to form a 3 1/2-inches circle.
- Place a pitted plum in the center of each circle and place a tsp of sugar into each plum.
- Roll and pinch the dough around the plum to seal.
- In a pan, add the lightly salted water and bring to a boil on medium heat.
- Add the dumplings into the boiling water and boil for about 5 minutes.
- With a slotted spoon, gently remove the dumplings and roll in the toasted bread crumbs.

Amount per serving (16 total)

Timing Information:

Preparation	1 h 30 m
Cooking	45 m
Total Time	2 h 15 m

Nutritional Information:

Calories	231 kcal
Fat	4 g
Carbohydrates	44.6g
Protein	5.3 g
Cholesterol	19 mg
Sodium	80 mg

* Percent Daily Values are based on a 2,000 calorie diet.

Easy Homemade Plum Cake

Ingredients

- 7 C. pitted and quartered plums
- 2/3 C. butter, softened
- 1 1/2 C. white sugar
- 2 eggs
- 3 C. sifted all-purpose flour
- 1 tbsp baking powder
- 1/2 tsp salt
- 2 C. milk
- 2 tsp vanilla extract
- 1 C. white sugar
- 1/2 C. butter, softened
- 1/4 C. all-purpose flour
- 1 tsp cinnamon

Directions

- Set your oven to 350 degrees F before doing anything else and grease a 13x9-inch baking dish.

- Arrange the plums into the bottom of the prepared baking dish.
- In a large bowl, add 2/3 C. of the butter, 1 1/2 C. of the white sugar and mix till a smooth and creamy mixture forms.
- Add the eggs, one at a time, beating continuously.
- Stir in 3 C. of the flour, baking powder and salt.
- Add the milk and vanilla extract and mix till a smooth mixture forms.
- Place the mixture over the plums evenly.
- In a bowl, add 1 C. of the sugar, 1/2 C. of the butter, 1/4 C. of the flour and cinnamon and mix till a crumbly topping forms.
- Spread the topping over the mixture.
- Cook in the oven for about 45-50 minutes or till a toothpick inserted in the center comes out clean.

Amount per serving (12 total)

Timing Information:

Preparation	30 m
Cooking	45 m
Total Time	1 h 15 m

Nutritional Information:

Calories	522 kcal
Fat	20.1 g
Carbohydrates	80.9g
Protein	6.8 g
Cholesterol	82 mg
Sodium	337 mg

* Percent Daily Values are based on a 2,000 calorie diet.

Cinnamon Clove and Plum Bread

Ingredients

- 1 C. vegetable oil
- 3 eggs
- 2 (6 oz.) jars plum baby food
- 2 C. white sugar
- 1 tsp red food coloring
- 2 C. all-purpose flour
- 1 tsp ground cloves
- 1 tsp ground cinnamon
- 1/2 tsp ground nutmeg
- 1/2 tsp salt
- 1/2 tsp baking soda
- 1 C. chopped walnuts
- 1 C. confectioners' sugar
- 2 1/2 tbsp lemon juice

Directions

- Set your oven to 350 degrees F before doing anything else and grease and flour bundt pan.
- In a large bowl, mix together the vegetable oil, white sugar, eggs, baby food and food coloring.
- In another bowl, mix together flour, cloves, cinnamon, nutmeg, salt, baking soda and nuts.
- Add the egg mixture into the flour mixture and mix till well combined.
- Transfer the mixture into the prepared bundt pan.
- Cook in the oven for about 50-60 minutes or till a toothpick inserted in the center comes out clean.
- Remove from the oven and cool for about 10 minutes before turning out onto wire rack to cool.
- In a bowl, mix together the confectioner's sugar and lemon juice.
- Brush the top of hot cake with the lemon mixture.

Amount per serving (12 total)

Timing Information:

Preparation	10 m
Cooking	1 h
Total Time	1 h 30 m

Nutritional Information:

Calories	510 kcal
Fat	26.2 g
Carbohydrates	66.7g
Protein	5.3 g
Cholesterol	46 mg
Sodium	170 mg

* Percent Daily Values are based on a 2,000 calorie diet.

German Plum Cake

(Kuchen)

Ingredients

Batter:

- 1/2 C. white sugar
- 2 tbsp margarine
- 2 eggs, beaten
- 1 C. all-purpose flour
- 1 tsp baking powder
- 1/4 tsp salt
- 1 tsp vanilla extract
- 10 Italian plums, halved and pitted

Topping:

- 1 C. white sugar
- 1/2 C. all-purpose flour
- 3 tbsp margarine, melted
- 1/2 tsp ground cinnamon

Directions

- Set your oven to 375 degrees F before doing anything else and grease and flour an 11x7-inch baking dish.
- In a bowl, add 1/2 C. of the sugar and 2 tbsp of the margarine and with an electric mixer, beat till smooth and creamy.
- Add the eggs, 1 C. of the flour, baking powder and salt and vanilla and mix till well combined.
- Transfer the mixture into the prepared baking dish and top with the plums, skin side-down.
- In a bowl, add 1 C. of the sugar, 1/2 C. of the flour, 3 tbsp of the margarine and cinnamon and mix till a crumbly mixture forms.
- Place the crumbly mixture over the plums.
- Cook in the oven for about 35 minutes.

Amount per serving (12 total)

Timing Information:

Preparation	15 m
Cooking	35 m
Total Time	50 m

Nutritional Information:

Calories	232 kcal
Fat	5.6 g
Carbohydrates	43.5g
Protein	3.1 g
Cholesterol	31 mg
Sodium	153 mg

* Percent Daily Values are based on a 2,000 calorie diet.

A Very Light Flan

Ingredients

- 2 C. plums, pitted and sliced
- 1 tbsp water (optional)
- 1 (.25 oz.) package unflavored pectin
- 1/2 C. hot water
- 1/2 C. white sugar
- 2 tbsp lemon juice
- 1/2 C. evaporated milk

Directions

- In a pan, add the plums on medium-low heat and simmer, covered for about 5-10 minutes, stirring occasionally.
- If the mixture becomes too thick or starts to burn, add a tbsp of water.
- Remove from the heat and keep aside to cool.
- In a bowl, add the pectin and 1/2 C. of the hot water and stir to dissolve.

- Add the cooled plums, sugar and lemon juice and mix till the pectin and sugar are dissolved.
- Refrigerate to chill for about 30 minutes.
- In a bowl, add the evaporated milk and with an electric mixer, beat till thick.
- Gently, add the whipped milk into the plum mixture and with electric mixer beat till fluffy and well combined.
- Refrigerate to chill for at least 3 hours before serving.

Amount per serving (5 total)

Timing Information:

Preparation	15 m
Cooking	5 m
Total Time	3 h 50 m

Nutritional Information:

Calories	148 kcal
Fat	2.1 g
Carbohydrates	30.6g
Protein	3.4 g
Cholesterol	7 mg
Sodium	30 mg

* Percent Daily Values are based on a 2,000 calorie diet.

Plum Jelly 101

Ingredients

- 4 1/2 C. pitted, chopped plums
- 1/2 C. water
- 7 1/2 C. white sugar
- 1/2 tsp butter (optional)
- 1 (1.75 oz.) package powdered fruit pectin
- 8 half-pint canning jars with lids and rings

Directions

- In a large pan, add the plums and water and bring to a boil.
- Reduce the heat to medium-low and simmer, covered for about 5 minutes.
- Stir in the sugar, then add the butter to reduce the foaming.
- Bring them to a full, rolling boil over high heat, stirring continuously.
- Immediately, stir in the pectin and bring to a full boil.
- Boil for about 1 minute, stirring continuously.
- Remove from the heat and skim off and discard any foam.

- Sterilize the jars and lids in boiling water for at least 5 minutes.
- Place the plum jam into the hot, sterilized jars, filling the jars to within 1/8-inch of the top.
- Run a knife around the insides of the jars to remove any air bubbles.
- With a moist paper towel, wipe the rims of the jars to remove any food residue.
- Top with lids and screw on rings.
- Place a rack in the bottom of a large pan and fill halfway with the water and bring to a boil on high heat.
- With a holder carefully, lower the jars into the pan, leave a 2-inch space between the jars.
- Bring the water to a full boil and process, covered for about 10 minutes.
- Remove the jars from the pan and place onto a wood surface, several inches apart to cool.
- After cooling, press the top of each lid with a finger, ensuring that the seal is tight.
- Store in a cool, dark area.
- Refrigerate opened jars for up to 3 weeks.

Amount per serving (128 total)

Timing Information:

Preparation	30 m
Cooking	20 m
Total Time	2 h 50 m

Nutritional Information:

Calories	48 kcal
Fat	0 g
Carbohydrates	12.4g
Protein	0 g
Cholesterol	1 mg
Sodium	1 mg

* Percent Daily Values are based on a 2,000 calorie diet.

How to Make Tapioca Pudding

Ingredients

- 12 plums, pitted and halved
- 1 C. white sugar
- 1/2 C. water
- 2 tbsp tapioca
- 1/2 tsp ground cinnamon
- 2 1/4 C. all-purpose baking mix
- 3 tbsp white sugar
- 2/3 C. milk
- 3 tbsp margarine, melted

Directions

- Set your oven to 350 degrees F before doing anything else.
- In a 2 quart baking dish, mix together the plums, 1 C. of the sugar, water, tapioca and cinnamon.
- Cook in the oven for about 25 minutes.
- Now, set the oven temperature to 450 degrees F.

- In a bowl, add the baking mix, 3 tbsp of the sugar, milk and melted margarine and mix till a biscuit dough forms.
- With spoonfuls, place the mixture over the plum mixture.
- Cook in the oven for about 10 minutes.
- Remove from the oven and keep aside to cool slightly before serving.

Amount per serving (6 total)

Timing Information:

Preparation	15 m
Cooking	35 m
Total Time	50 m

Nutritional Information:

Calories	468 kcal
Fat	13 g
Carbohydrates	86.1g
Protein	5.1 g
Cholesterol	2 mg
Sodium	641 mg

* Percent Daily Values are based on a 2,000 calorie diet.

Rustic Pie

Ingredients

- 3 C. all-purpose flour
- 3/4 C. white sugar
- 2 1/2 tsp baking powder
- 1/8 tsp salt
- 2/3 C. butter
- 2 eggs
- 1 tsp vanilla extract
- 3 tbsp milk
- 1/2 tsp lemon zest
- 1/2 C. all-purpose flour
- 1/4 C. packed brown sugar
- 1/2 tsp ground cinnamon
- 1/4 tsp salt
- 1/3 C. chopped hazelnuts
- 1 tsp lemon zest
- 3 tbsp butter
- 5 C. plums, pitted and sliced
- 1 C. white sugar

- 1/4 C. all-purpose flour
- 1 tsp ground cinnamon
- 1/2 tsp ground nutmeg

Directions

- Set your oven to 375 degrees F before doing anything else.
- For crust in a large bowl, mix together 3 C. of the flour, 3/4 C. of the white sugar, baking powder and 1/8 tsp of the salt.
- With a pastry cutter, cut in 2/3 C. butter till pieces are the size of small peas.
- Add the eggs, vanilla extract, milk and lemon zest and mix till just combined.
- Refrigerate the dough till serving.
- For streusel topping in a bowl mix together 1/2 C. of the flour, brown sugar, 1/2 tsp of the cinnamon, 1/4 tsp of the salt, chopped nuts and grated lemon zest.
- Add the butter and with the fingers, mix till all the Ingredients are well combined.
- For fruit filling in a large bowl, add the pitted and sliced fruit.
- In a small bowl, mix together the remaining sugar, flour, cinnamon, and nutmeg.

- Place the sugar mixture over the fruit and stir gently until all fruit is evenly coated.
- Roll out pie crust and arrange in a 9-inch pie pan.
- Trim and flute the edges.
- Place the fruit filling over the crust and top with the streusel topping evenly.
- Cook in the oven for about 45-55 minutes.
- Serve warm or at room temperature.

Amount per serving (8 total)

Timing Information:

Preparation	30 m
Cooking	1 h
Total Time	1 h 30 m

Nutritional Information:

Calories	685 kcal
Fat	24.9 g
Carbohydrates	109.1g
Protein	9.5 g
Cholesterol	99 mg
Sodium	424 mg

* Percent Daily Values are based on a 2,000 calorie diet.

Moist Homemade Plum Lemon Cake

Ingredients

- 3 eggs, whites and yolks separated
- 1/2 C. butter, softened
- 1/2 C. white sugar
- 1 tsp lemon zest
- 1 C. all-purpose flour
- 1/2 tsp baking powder
- 1 1/4 C. plums, pitted and sliced

Directions

- Set your oven to 375 degrees F before doing anything else and grease and flour a 9-inch tube pan.
- In a small bowl, add the egg whites and beat till stiff peaks form.
- In a large bowl, add the butter and sugar and beat till creamy and smooth.
- Add the egg yolks and lemon zest and beat to combine.
- In another bowl, mix together the flour and baking powder.
- Add the flour mixture into the butter mixture and mix to combine.

- Gently fold in the egg whites.
- Transfer the mixture into the prepared pan evenly and top with the plums, skin side down, attractively.
- Cook in the oven for about 40 minutes or till a toothpick inserted in the center comes out clean.
- Remove from the oven and cool for about 10 minutes before turning out onto wire rack to cool completely.

Amount per serving (12 total)

Timing Information:

Preparation	10 m
Cooking	1 h
Total Time	1 h 10 m

Nutritional Information:

Calories	164 kcal
Fat	9.1 g
Carbohydrates	18.4g
Protein	2.9 g
Cholesterol	67 mg
Sodium	93 mg

* Percent Daily Values are based on a 2,000 calorie diet.

Traditional French Dessert

Ingredients

- 6 tbsp white sugar, divided
- 14 Italian prune plums, halved and pitted
- 3 eggs
- 1 1/3 C. milk
- 2/3 C. all-purpose flour
- 1 1/2 tsp grated lemon zest
- 2 tsp vanilla
- 1 pinch salt
- 1/2 tsp ground cinnamon
- 2 tbsp confectioners' sugar

Directions

- Set your oven to 375 degrees F before doing anything else and butter a 10-inch pie plate, then sprinkle 1 tbsp of the sugar over the bottom.
- In the bottom of the prepared pan, place the plum halves evenly, cut side down and sprinkle with 2 tbsp of the sugar.

- In a blender, add the remaining 3 tbsp of the sugar, eggs, milk, flour, lemon zest, cinnamon, vanilla and salt and pulse till smooth.
- Place the pureed mixture over the plum evenly.
- Cook in the oven for about 50-60 minute.
- Remove from the oven and keep aside for about 5 minutes before slicing.
- Dust with the confectioner's sugar before serving.

Amount per serving (8 total)

Timing Information:

Preparation	10 m
Cooking	1 h
Total Time	1 h 10 m

Nutritional Information:

Calories	186 kcal
Fat	3.1 g
Carbohydrates	34.9g
Protein	5.6 g
Cholesterol	73 mg
Sodium	63 mg

* Percent Daily Values are based on a 2,000 calorie diet.

Jalapeno Plum Chipotle Sauce

Ingredients

- 5 quarts very ripe plums, pitted
- 4 cloves garlic, pressed
- 1 onion, finely chopped
- 6 C. white sugar
- 1/2 C. apple cider vinegar
- 2 tbsp Southwest chipotle seasoning
- 1 tbsp roasted garlic seasoning
- 1 jalapeno pepper, finely chopped (remove seeds for milder flavor if desired)
- 7 tsp salt
- 1 tsp liquid smoke flavoring (optional)
- 8 half-pint canning jars with lids and rings

Directions

- Arrange a colander over a large bowl.

- Place the plums in the colander and with gloved hands, squeeze the plums in the colander, forcing the juice through the holes of the colander.
- Discard the spent pulp, and repeat to produce 8 C. of the plum juice.
- In a small pan, add 3/4 C. of the plum juice, garlic and onion on medium heat and bring to a boil.
- Reduce the heat to medium-low and simmer for about 5 minutes.
- In a large pan, add the juice-onion mixture with the remaining 7 1/2 C. of plum juice, sugar, apple cider vinegar, Southwest chipotle seasoning, roasted garlic seasoning, jalapeño pepper, salt and liquid smoke flavoring and stir till the sugar is dissolved.
- Bring to a boil on medium heat.
- Reduce heat to a simmer and cook for about 1 1/2 hours, stirring occasionally.
- Sterilize the jars and lids in boiling water for at least 5 minutes.
- Place the sauce into the hot, sterilized jars, filling the jars to within 1/4-inch of the top.
- Run a knife around the insides of the jars to remove any air bubbles.
- With a moist paper towel, wipe the rims of the jars to remove any food residue.
- Top with the lids and screw on rings.

- Place a rack in the bottom of a large pan and fill halfway with the water.
- Bring to a boil on high heat.
- With a holder carefully, lower the jars into the pan, leaving a 2-inch space between the jars.
- Bring the water to a full boil and process, covered for about 10 minutes.
- Remove the jars from the pan and place onto a wood surface, several inches apart to cool.
- After cooling, press the top of each lid with a finger, ensuring that the seal is tight.
- Store in a cool, dark area.

Amount per serving (128 total)

Timing Information:

Preparation	1 h
Cooking	1 h 40 m
Total Time	4 h 40 m

Nutritional Information:

Calories	50 kcal
Fat	0.1 g
Carbohydrates	12.5g
Protein	0.2 g
Cholesterol	0 mg
Sodium	179 mg

* Percent Daily Values are based on a 2,000 calorie diet.

Persian Inspired Cardamom and Plum Jam

Ingredients

- 5 lb. fresh Damask plums
- 1 C. water
- 12 whole cardamom pods
- 4 C. white sugar
- 1/4 tsp butter

Directions

- Rinse the plum and remove the stems.
- In a thick-bottomed and deep pan, add the plums, water and cardamom pods and bring them to a gentle boil on medium heat.
- Reduce the heat to low and simmer, uncovered for about 1 1/2 hours.
- Remove from the heat and keep aside to cool.
- Place the plums in a colander and with your hands, press the cooled plums to extract the juice in a large bowl.

- Pick up the pit-and-fruit slurry in the colander by small handfuls and squeeze the plum pulp and skins gently into the bowl with the syrup.
- Return the plum juice in the pan with the sugar and butter on very low heat.
- Simmer for about 4 hours.
- Place the hot jam into hot, sterile jars.
- Wipe the rims clean and place sterile lids on, then tighten the screw caps.
- Keep the jars in room temperature to cool.

Amount per serving (100 total)

Timing Information:

Preparation	
Cooking	5 h 30 m
Total Time	7 h 30 m

Nutritional Information:

Calories	42 kcal
Fat	0.1 g
Carbohydrates	10.7g
Protein	0.2 g
Cholesterol	1 mg
Sodium	1 mg

* Percent Daily Values are based on a 2,000 calorie diet.

New Age Plum Cake

Ingredients

- 1/2 C. whole wheat flour
- 1/2 C. all-purpose flour
- 1 tsp baking powder
- 1/2 tsp salt
- 1/2 C. butter, softened
- 3/4 C. white sugar
- 2 eggs
- 3 plums, pitted and sliced
- 1 tbsp white sugar
- 1 tsp cinnamon

Directions

- Set your oven to 350 degrees F before doing anything else and grease an 11x7-inch baking dish.
- In a bowl, mix together the whole wheat flour, white flour, baking powder and salt.

- In another large bowl, add the butter and 3/4 C. of the sugar and beat till creamy.
- Add the eggs, one at a time, beating till well combined.
- Add the flour mixture into the egg mixture and gently, mix till just combined.
- Transfer the mixture into the prepared baking dish and with the sliced plums.
- Sprinkle 1 tbsp sugar and cinnamon over the plums.
- Cook in the oven for about 50-55 minutes or till a toothpick inserted in the center comes out clean.

Amount per serving (8 total)

Timing Information:

Preparation	30 m
Cooking	50 m
Total Time	1 h 20 m

Nutritional Information:

Calories	264 kcal
Fat	13 g
Carbohydrates	35g
Protein	3.7 g
Cholesterol	77 mg
Sodium	306 mg

* Percent Daily Values are based on a 2,000 calorie diet.

Agave Butter

Ingredients

- 2 lb. plums, pitted and sliced
- 2 lb. apples - peeled, cored, and chopped
- 1 C. apple juice
- 1 C. agave nectar
- 1 1/2 tsp ground cinnamon
- 1 tsp ground cloves
- 1 tsp ground nutmeg
- 1 tsp ground ginger

Directions

- In a large pan, mix together the plums, apples and apple juice on medium heat and simmer, covered for about 15 minutes.
- With a potato masher, mash the fruit.
- Stir in the agave nectar, cinnamon, cloves, nutmeg and ginger and simmer for about 30-50 minutes, stirring occasionally.
- Remove from heat and keep aside for at least 1 hour to cool completely.

- Place the apple butter into jars and cover with a lid.
- Refrigerate for up to 3 weeks or freeze for up to 6 months.

Amount per serving (40 total)

Timing Information:

Preparation	15 m
Cooking	45 m
Total Time	2 h

Nutritional Information:

Calories	50 kcal
Fat	0.2 g
Carbohydrates	13g
Protein	0.2 g
Cholesterol	0 mg
Sodium	1 mg

* Percent Daily Values are based on a 2,000 calorie diet.

Fruity Plum Rolls German Style

Ingredients

- 1 C. chopped almonds
- 1 1/3 C. cream cheese
- 1/2 C. milk
- 1/2 C. vegetable oil
- 1 pinch salt
- 5/8 C. white sugar
- 1 tsp ground cinnamon
- 4 C. all-purpose flour
- 1/4 C. baking powder
- 7/8 C. plum butter
- 1 3/4 lb. plums, pitted and diced
- 2 tbsp butter, melted

Directions

- Set your oven to 350 degrees F before doing anything else and grease a 10-inch spring form pan.

- Heat a skillet on medium-high heat and toast the almonds till browned.
- Remove from heat and keep aside to cool.
- In a bowl, add the cream cheese, milk, oil, salt, sugar and cinnamon and beat till well combined.
- Add the flour and baking powder and knead the mixture till smooth.
- Place the dough onto a lightly floured surface and roll into a 20-inch square.
- Spread the plum butter, plums, and toasted almonds over the dough and roll tightly like a jelly roll.
- Cut the dough roll into 12 equal sized slices.
- Place the rolls in the prepared pan in a single layer and coat the top of each roll with the butter.
- Cook in the oven for about 40-55 minutes.

Amount per serving (12 total)

Timing Information:

Preparation	40 m
Cooking	50 m
Total Time	1 h 30 m

Nutritional Information:

Calories	499 kcal
Fat	24.9 g
Carbohydrates	62.7g
Protein	8.8 g
Cholesterol	34 mg
Sodium	618 mg

* Percent Daily Values are based on a 2,000 calorie diet.

Plum Poblano Salsa

Ingredients

- 2 large tomatoes, diced
- 1/2 small red onion, diced
- 4 plums, pitted and diced
- 1 Poblano chili pepper, seeded and finely chopped
- 8 sprigs fresh cilantro, chopped (optional)
- 1 tsp minced garlic
- 1 tsp lime juice
- 1/2 tsp salt
- 1/4 tsp freshly ground black pepper
- 1/4 tsp chili powder

Directions

- In a large bowl, mix together the tomatoes, onion, plums, Poblano chili pepper, cilantro, garlic, lime juice, salt, black pepper and chili powder.
- With a plastic wrap, cover the bowl and refrigerate for at least 1 hour.

Amount per serving (12 total)

Timing Information:

Preparation	
Cooking	15 m
Total Time	1 h 15 m

Nutritional Information:

Calories	20 kcal
Fat	0.2 g
Carbohydrates	4.6g
Protein	0.6 g
Cholesterol	0 mg
Sodium	101 mg

* Percent Daily Values are based on a 2,000 calorie diet.

Plum No Sugar Butter

Ingredients

- 1 C. finely chopped, peeled peaches
- 1 C. pitted, chopped plums
- 1 tbsp water
- 1/2 tsp ground cinnamon
- 1/2 tsp ground ginger
- 1/2 C. granular no-calorie sucralose sweetener (such as Splenda(R))

Directions

- In a microwave-safe glass bowl, mix together the peaches, plums and water and microwave on high for about 15 minutes, stirring after every 3 minutes.
- Stir in the cinnamon, ginger and sweetener.
- Place the fruit butter into a jar and refrigerate, covered before serving.

Amount per serving (16 total)

Timing Information:

Preparation	10 m
Cooking	15 m
Total Time	2 h 25 m

Nutritional Information:

Calories	10 kcal
Fat	0 g
Carbohydrates	2.4g
Protein	0.1 g
Cholesterol	0 mg
Sodium	1 mg

* Percent Daily Values are based on a 2,000 calorie diet.

Asian Inspired Chicken

Ingredients

- 1 (2.5 lb.) whole chicken, cut into pieces
- salt and ground black pepper to taste
- 2/3 C. plum jam
- 1 1/2 tsp ground black pepper
- 1 1/2 tsp minced fresh ginger root
- 1 1/4 tsp prepared horseradish (optional)

Directions

- Set your oven to 350 degrees F before doing anything else and grease a baking sheet.
- Season the chicken pieces with the salt and pepper.
- In the prepared baking sheet, place the chicken, skin-side-up.
- Cook in the oven for about 20 minutes.
- Meanwhile in a bowl, mix together the plum jam, 1 1/2 tsp of the pepper, ginger and horseradish.
- Remove the chicken from the oven and coat the plum glaze.
- Cook in the oven for about 20-30 minutes more.

Amount per serving (4 total)

Timing Information:

Preparation	10 m
Cooking	40 m
Total Time	50 m

Nutritional Information:

Calories	496 kcal
Fat	21.1 g
Carbohydrates	37.6g
Protein	37.9 g
Cholesterol	120 mg
Sodium	217 mg

* Percent Daily Values are based on a 2,000 calorie diet.

Autumnal Warm Baked Plums

Ingredients

- 4 plums, halved and pitted
- 1/2 C. orange juice
- 2 tbsp packed brown sugar
- 1/2 tsp ground cinnamon
- 1/8 tsp ground nutmeg
- 1/8 tsp cumin
- 1/8 tsp ground cardamom
- 1/4 C. toasted slivered almonds (optional)

Directions

- Set your oven to 400 degrees F before doing anything else and grease a baking dish.
- In a bowl, add the orange juice, brown sugar, cinnamon, nutmeg, cumin, and cardamom and beat till well combined.
- In the bottom of the prepared baking dish, place the plums, cut-side up in a single layer and drizzle with the orange juice mixture evenly.

- Cook in the oven for about 20 minutes.
- Serve with a topping of the toasted almonds.

Amount per serving (4 total)

Timing Information:

Preparation	15 m
Cooking	20 m
Total Time	35 m

Nutritional Information:

Calories	113 kcal
Fat	3.7 g
Carbohydrates	19.1g
Protein	2.1 g
Cholesterol	0 mg
Sodium	3 mg

* Percent Daily Values are based on a 2,000 calorie diet.

Gourmet Chicken

Ingredients

- 1 C. uncooked long grain white rice
- 2 C. water
- 2/3 C. plum sauce
- 1/2 C. light corn syrup
- 2 tbsp soy sauce
- 2 cloves garlic, minced
- 4 packets chicken bouillon granules
- 2 tbsp vegetable oil
- 4 skinless, boneless chicken breast halves - cut into bite-size pieces
- 4 tbsp cornstarch
- 3/4 tsp minced fresh ginger root
- 2 C. snow peas, trimmed
- 1 C. sliced fresh mushrooms

Directions

- In a pan, add the rice and water and bring to a boil.
- Reduce the heat to low and simmer, covered for about 20 minutes.

- In a bowl, mix together the plum sauce, corn syrup, soy sauce, garlic and bouillon.
- Coat the chicken with the cornstarch evenly.
- In a skillet, heat the oil on medium heat and cook the chicken for about 5 minutes.
- Stir in the ginger, snow peas and mushrooms and cook till tender.
- Stir in the plum sauce mixture and cook till heated completely.

Amount per serving (6 total)

Timing Information:

Preparation	15 m
Cooking	25 m
Total Time	40 m

Nutritional Information:

Calories	432 kcal
Fat	7.4 g
Carbohydrates	70.9g
Protein	20.5 g
Cholesterol	41 mg
Sodium	1283 mg

* Percent Daily Values are based on a 2,000 calorie diet.

Pretty Cake

Ingredients

- 1 1/4 C. all-purpose flour
- 1 1/2 tsp baking powder
- 1/4 tsp salt
- 3 tbsp margarine
- 1/4 C. brown sugar
- 1/3 C. margarine
- 1 C. white sugar
- 1 egg
- 1 tsp vanilla extract
- 3/4 C. milk
- 4 black plums, pitted and thinly sliced
- 3/4 C. blueberries

Directions

- Set your oven to 350 degrees F before doing anything else and grease a 9-inch cake pan.
- In a bowl, mix together the flour, baking powder and salt.

- In the prepared cake pan, mix together 3 tbsp of the margarine and brown sugar.
- Place pan inside the preheated oven till the margarine melts and begins to bubble.
- In a large bowl, add 1/3 C. of the margarine and 1 C. of the white sugar and beat till light and fluffy.
- Add the egg and beat till well combined.
- Stir in the vanilla.
- Add the flour mixture alternately with the milk and beat till just combined.
- Place the plums around the edges of the prepared pan, overlapping slightly and arrange the blueberries in the center.
- Place the flour mixture over the fruit evenly.
- Cook in the oven for about 40 minutes, or till a toothpick inserted in the center comes out clean.
- Remove from the oven and cool for about 15 minutes before serving.

Amount per serving (12 total)

Timing Information:

Preparation	30 m
Cooking	40 m
Total Time	1 h 10 m

Nutritional Information:

Calories	229 kcal
Fat	8.8 g
Carbohydrates	35.9g
Protein	2.7 g
Cholesterol	17 mg
Sodium	196 mg

* Percent Daily Values are based on a 2,000 calorie diet.

Thursday's Dinner Plum Chicken With Rice

Ingredients

- 1 1/2 C. water
- 1 C. uncooked basmati rice, rinsed and drained
- 3/4 lb. plums, pitted and chopped
- 1/2 medium red onion, minced
- 3 habanero peppers, seeded and minced
- 3 tbsp minced fresh cilantro
- 1 tsp sugar
- 3/4 lb. boneless, skinless chicken breasts
- 2 tsp fresh rosemary, minced
- salt and pepper to taste
- 2 tsp vegetable oil

Directions

- In a medium pan, place the water and rice and bring to a boil.
- Reduce the heat and simmer, covered for about 20 minutes.

- Remove from the heat and fluff with a fork.
- In a bowl, mix together the plums, onion, habanero peppers, cilantro and sugar.
- Refrigerate, covered for about 30 minutes.
- Meanwhile, season the chicken with the fresh rosemary, salt, and pepper.
- In a large skillet, heat the vegetable oil on medium-high heat and cook the chicken breasts for about 1 minute per side.
- Reduce heat to medium and cook the chicken about 5 minutes per side.
- Serve over rice with plum salsa.

Amount per serving (2 total)

Timing Information:

Preparation	30 m
Cooking	20 m
Total Time	50 m

Nutritional Information:

Calories	660 kcal
Fat	8.4 g
Carbohydrates	98.5g
Protein	48.2 g
Cholesterol	99 mg
Sodium	115 mg

* Percent Daily Values are based on a 2,000 calorie diet.

Mediterrean Plum Salad

Ingredients

- 2 C. escarole - torn, rinsed and dried
- 2 C. romaine lettuce - torn, washed and dried
- 2 C. Bibb lettuce, rinsed and torn
- 12 slices plum tomato
- 1/2 C. balsamic vinegar
- 1 tbsp olive oil
- 1 tbsp grated Parmesan cheese
- 2 cloves garlic, minced
- 1 tbsp lemon juice
- 1/4 C. low fat, low sodium chicken broth
- salt and pepper to taste

Directions

- In a salad bowl, mix together the escarole, romaine, Bibb lettuce and tomatoes.

- In another bowl, add the vinegar, olive oil, cheese, garlic lemon juice, chicken broth and salt and pepper and beat till well combined.
- Place the dressing over the salad and toss to coat well.
- Serve immediately.

Amount per serving (6 total)

Timing Information:

Preparation	
Cooking	20 m
Total Time	20 m

Nutritional Information:

Calories	53 kcal
Fat	2.7 g
Carbohydrates	6.5g
Protein	1.5 g
Cholesterol	1 mg
Sodium	42 mg

* Percent Daily Values are based on a 2,000 calorie diet.

Lunch Box Chicken

Ingredients

- 1 tbsp olive oil
- 2 (6 oz.) skinless, boneless chicken breast halves
- Salt and pepper to taste
- 2 pieces cornbread, crumbled
- 2 slices cooked bacon, crumbled
- 2 tbsp minced celery
- 2 tbsp minced onion
- 2 tbsp butter, melted
- 1/4 C. chicken stock
- 1/3 C. chicken stock
- 1/3 C. plum jam

Directions

- Set your oven to 350 degrees F before doing anything else.
- With a paring knife, cut a pocket into the side of each breast.
- In a skillet, heat the olive oil on high heat and sear the chicken till lightly browned from both sides.

- Remove from the heat and keep aside.
- In a bowl, mix together the cornbread, bacon, celery, onion, butter, and 1/4 C. of the chicken stock.
- Stuff each chicken breast with the cornbread mixture.
- Cook in the oven for about 25 minutes.
- Meanwhile in a pan, add 1/3 C. of the chicken stock and bring to a simmer.
- Stir in the plum jam and simmer on medium-low heat till most of the chicken stock is absorbed.
- Place the plum glaze over the chicken breasts and cook in the oven for about 10 minutes more.

Amount per serving (2 total)

Timing Information:

Preparation	15 m
Cooking	40 m
Total Time	55 m

Nutritional Information:

Calories	684 kcal
Fat	30 g
Carbohydrates	61.1g
Protein	42.1 g
Cholesterol	156 mg
Sodium	867 mg

* Percent Daily Values are based on a 2,000 calorie diet.

Artisanal Plum Roasted Chicken

Ingredients

- 3 (1 1/2 lb.) Cornish game hens
- 1/2 tsp crushed red pepper flakes
- 3/4 C. plum jam
- 1 (1.25 oz.) envelope dry onion soup mix
- 2 kiwifruit, peeled and sliced, for garnish

Directions

- In a slow cooker, place the game hens and sprinkle with the red pepper flakes.
- In a bowl, add the plum jam and onion soup mix and stir till well combined.
- Reserve about 1/4 C. of the jam mixture and refrigerate.
- Coat the game hens with the remaining jam mixture.
- Set the slow cooker on Low and cook, covered for about 7 hours.
- Brush the reserved glaze over the hens and cook on Low for about 1 hour more.
- Serve the hens with a garnishing of the kiwifruit slices.

Amount per serving (6 total)

Timing Information:

Preparation	10 m
Cooking	8 h
Total Time	8 h 10 m

Nutritional Information:

Calories	437 kcal
Fat	21.3 g
Carbohydrates	35g
Protein	26.4 g
Cholesterol	151 mg
Sodium	589 mg

* Percent Daily Values are based on a 2,000 calorie diet.

Cobbler French Style

Ingredients

- 2 C. sliced fresh peaches
- 2 C. sliced fresh nectarines
- 2 C. pitted and quartered plums
- 1 tsp cornstarch
- 1 C. currant jelly
- 1/2 tsp apple pie spice
- 1/8 tsp white pepper
- 1 (16.3 oz.) can refrigerated flaky biscuits (such as Pillsbury Grands!(R))
- 1/4 C. white sugar
- 1/4 tsp ground cinnamon

Directions

- Set your oven to 350 degrees F before doing anything else and grease a 13x8-inch baking dish.
- In a large bowl, add the peach, nectarine, plum slices and cornstarch and gently toss to coat.

- Add the currant jelly, apple pie spice and white pepper and with your hands, lightly mix to coat the fruit with the jelly and seasonings.
- Place the fruit mixture into the prepared baking dish evenly.
- Pop open the can of biscuits and cut them in half.
- Place the biscuit dough halves on top of the fruit.
- In a small bowl, mix together the sugar and cinnamon.
- Sprinkle the cinnamon sugar over the biscuit dough evenly.
- Cook in the oven for about 20-25 minutes.
- Remove from the oven and cool for about 20 minutes onto wire rack.

Amount per serving (8 total)

Timing Information:

Preparation	20 m
Cooking	20 m
Total Time	1 h

Nutritional Information:

Calories	358 kcal
Fat	8 g
Carbohydrates	69.3g
Protein	4.5 g
Cholesterol	1 mg
Sodium	571 mg

* Percent Daily Values are based on a 2,000 calorie diet.

Healthy Fruit Medley Crumble

Ingredients

- 3 apples - peeled, cored and sliced
- 3 fresh peaches - peeled, pitted, and sliced
- 3 ripe plums, peeled, pitted and sliced
- 4 large strawberries, sliced
- 1 tbsp white sugar (optional)
- 1/2 tsp ground cinnamon (optional)
- 1/2 C. water
- 1/2 C. melted butter
- 1 C. white sugar
- 1/2 C. apricot nectar
- 1 C. all-purpose flour
- 1/2 C. quick-cooking rolled oats
- 1/2 C. graham cracker crumbs
- 1 tbsp ground cinnamon

Directions

- Set your oven to 350 degrees F before doing anything else and grease a 13x9-inch baking dish.
- In a large bowl, mix together the apples, peaches, plums and strawberries.
- In the bottom of the prepared baking dish, spread the fruit mixture evenly.
- Sprinkle with 1 tbsp of the sugar and 1/2 tsp of the cinnamon and drizzle with the water.
- In a bowl, add the butter, 1 C. of the sugar, apricot nectar, flour, rolled oats, graham cracker crumbs and 1 tbsp of the cinnamon and mix till a crumbly mixture forms.
- Spread the crumbly mixture over the fruit evenly.
- Cook in the oven for about 45 minutes.

Amount per serving (8 total)

Timing Information:

Preparation	15 m
Cooking	45 m
Total Time	1 h

Nutritional Information:

Calories	365 kcal
Fat	12.8 g
Carbohydrates	61.8g
Protein	3.3 g
Cholesterol	31 mg
Sodium	126 mg

* Percent Daily Values are based on a 2,000 calorie diet.

Best Breakfast Muffins

Ingredients

- 1 1/2 C. chopped fresh plums
- 1/4 C. water, or as needed
- 1 egg
- 1/4 C. molasses
- 1 C. oat bran
- 1 C. rolled oats
- 1 C. whole wheat flour
- 2 tsp baking powder
- 1/2 tsp baking soda
- 1 tbsp ground cinnamon

Directions

- Set your oven to 375 degrees F before doing anything else and lightly, grease 12 cups of a muffin pan.
- In a bowl, add the plums and enough water just to cover the plums.
- Add the egg and molasses and mix till well combined.

- In another bowl, mix together the oat bran, rolled oats, whole wheat flour, baking powder, baking soda and cinnamon.
- Add the plum mixture into the oat mixture and mix till just moistened.
- Transfer the mixture into the prepared muffin cups evenly.
- Cook in the oven for about 15 minutes or till a toothpick inserted in the center comes out clean.
- Remove from the oven and cool for about 10 minutes before turning out onto wire rack to cool completely.

Amount per serving (12 total)

Timing Information:

Preparation	15 m
Cooking	15 m
Total Time	30 m

Nutritional Information:

Calories	116 kcal
Fat	1.7 g
Carbohydrates	25.2g
Protein	4.3 g
Cholesterol	16 mg
Sodium	143 mg

* Percent Daily Values are based on a 2,000 calorie diet.

Richly Spiced Raisin and Plum Chutney

Ingredients

- 3 1/2 C. purple plums, seeds removed
- 1 C. brown sugar
- 1 C. sugar
- 3/4 C. cider vinegar
- 1 C. golden seedless raisins
- 2 tsp salt
- 1/3 C. chopped onion
- 1 clove garlic, minced
- 2 tsp mustard seeds
- 3 tbsp chopped crystallized ginger
- 3/4 tsp cayenne

Directions

- In a large pan, add the sugars and vinegar and bring to a boil, stirring till the sugars dissolves.
- Stir in the remaining Ingredients and bring to a boil.

- Reduce the heat and simmer for about 45-50 minutes, stirring occasionally.
- Place into the hot sterilized jars and seal.

Servings per Recipe: 1

Timing Information:

| Preparation | 20 mins |
| Total Time | 1 hr 10 mins |

Nutritional Information:

Calories	567.7
Fat	1.0g
Cholesterol	0.0mg
Sodium	1190.1mg
Carbohydrates	142.6g
Protein	2.4g

* Percent Daily Values are based on a 2,000 calorie diet.

3-Ingredient Jam

Ingredients

- 5 C. plums, pitted and diced
- 4 C. sugar
- 1 C. water

Directions

- In a large pan, mix together all the Ingredients and bring to a boil, stirring till the sugar dissolves.
- Cook rapidly almost to gelling point, stirring occasionally.
- Place into hot jars, leaving 1/4-inch head space.
- Seal with two-piece lid caps.
- Process for about 15 minutes in a boiling water canner.

Servings per Recipe: 1

Timing Information:

Preparation	20 mins
Total Time	50 mins

Nutritional Information:

Calories	631.9
Fat	0.4g
Cholesterol	0.0mg
Sodium	2.7mg
Carbohydrates	162.5g
Protein	1.0g

* Percent Daily Values are based on a 2,000 calorie diet.

Tempting Plums

Ingredients

- 1 large vanilla bean
- 1/4 C. sugar
- 2 C. unpeeled pitted plums, halved
- 1 1/2 tsp lemon juice
- 2 tsp margarine

Directions

- Set your oven to 400 degrees F before doing anything else.
- Cut the vanilla bean in half lengthwise.
- Scrape seeds into a small bowl and discard bean.
- Add the sugar and stir well.
- In a 1 quart baking dish, add the plums, sugar mixture and lemon juice and gently toss to coat.
- Top the margarine in the shape of dots.
- Cover the baking dish and cook in the oven for about 20 minutes.

Servings per Recipe: 4

Timing Information:

Preparation	10 mins
Total Time	30 mins

Nutritional Information:

Calories	103.6
Fat	2.1g
Cholesterol	0.0mg
Sodium	22.3mg
Carbohydrates	22.0g
Protein	0.6g

* Percent Daily Values are based on a 2,000 calorie diet.

I ♥ Plum Jam

Ingredients

- 1 1/2 kg damson plums
- 2 -3 C. water
- 4 -6 C. sugar

Directions

- Wash and pick over the plums.
- In a pan, add the plums and water and bring to a boil.
- Cook for about 15 minutes, stirring continuously.
- Remove from the heat and keep aside to cool completely.
- Remove the pits.
- Meanwhile, place the jars into a canning kettle and cover with water to one inch above the tops of the jars, then bring to a boil.
- Boil for about 10 minutes to sterilize.
- Return the plums to the jam pan and bring to a boil.
- Add the sugar and stir to dissolve.
- Boil the jam for about 20 minutes.

- Remove from the heat and stir and skim for about 5 minutes.
- Place into the hot sterilized jars and seal with lids.
- Place the jars of jam back in boiling water bath and boil for about 5 minutes.
- Let cool and store when the jars have sealed.

Servings per Recipe: 112

Timing Information:

| Preparation | 15 mins |
| Total Time | 1 hr |

Nutritional Information:

Calories	33.8
Fat	0.0g
Cholesterol	0.0mg
Sodium	0.2mg
Carbohydrates	8.6g
Protein	0.0g

* Percent Daily Values are based on a 2,000 calorie diet.

Shining ★ Muffins

Ingredients

- 2 firm plums
- 2 C. flour
- 1 C. sugar
- 1 tbsp baking powder
- 1 tsp salt
- 4 tbsp melted butter
- 1/4 C. oil
- 3/4 C. milk
- 1 tsp vanilla extract
- cinnamon, for dusting muffin tops

Directions

- Set your oven to 350 degrees F before doing anything else and lightly, grease 6 large cups of a muffin pan.
- Peel and cut each plum into 6 slices.
- In a bowl, sift together the flour, sugar, baking powder and salt.

- Make a well in the center of the flour mixture.
- Add the melted butter, oil, milk and vanilla extract in the well and with your hands, mix till just combined.
- Transfer the mixture into the prepared muffin cups evenly.
- Insert 2 plum wedges into each muffin and sprinkle with the cinnamon.
- Cook in the oven for about 30 minutes or till a toothpick inserted in the center comes out clean.
- Remove from the oven and cool for about 5 minutes before turning out onto wire rack to cool completely.

Servings per Recipe: 1

Timing Information:

Preparation	15 mins
Total Time	45 mins

Nutritional Information:

Calories	461.6
Fat	18.3g
Cholesterol	24.6mg
Sodium	652.8mg
Carbohydrates	69.7g
Protein	5.5g

* Percent Daily Values are based on a 2,000 calorie diet.

LATIN ORANGE BUTTERY FLAN

Ingredients

- 3/4 C. white sugar
- 1/4 C. soft butter
- 2 eggs
- 1 C. all-purpose flour
- 1 tsp baking powder
- 1 tsp grated orange rind
- 1/4 C. low-fat milk
- 2 C. halved pitted fresh plums

TOPPING

- 1/2 C. brown sugar
- 1 tsp cinnamon

Directions

- Set your oven to 355 degrees F before doing anything else and grease a 10-inch spring form pan.

- In a bowl, add the sugar and butter and beat till creamy.
- Add the eggs and beat well.
- In another bowl, mix together the flour, baking powder and rind.
- Add the flour mixture into the egg mixture alternately with milk, making 3 additions of flour and 2 of milk.
- Transfer the mixture into the prepared pan and top with the plums, cut side down in circles, gently press into the mixture.
- For topping in a small bowl, mix together the sugar and cinnamon.
- Sprinkle the topping mixture over the fruit.
- Cook in the oven for about 45-55 minutes.

Servings per Recipe: 10

Timing Information:

Preparation	25 mins
Total Time	1 hr 10 mins

Nutritional Information:

Calories	219.1
Fat	5.8g
Cholesterol	54.8mg
Sodium	90.2mg
Carbohydrates	39.7g
Protein	3.0g

* Percent Daily Values are based on a 2,000 calorie diet.

Friday Night Plum Steak

Ingredients

- 1.5 lbs rump steak
- 2/3 C. plum sauce
- 1 tbsp soy sauce
- 1 garlic clove, crushed
- 1 tsp fresh ginger, grated
- 1/2 tsp fresh red chili, chopped
- 2 tsp sugar
- 2 tsp dry sherry
- 2 tsp corn flour
- 2 tbsp oil
- 2 tsp corn flour, extra
- ½ C. water
- 1 small beef stock cube, crumbled

Directions

- Trim the steak and slice thinly.

- In a large bowl, mix together the steak slices, sauces, garlic, ginger, red chili, sugar, sherry and corn flour.
- Refrigerate, covered to marinate for at least 30 minutes or overnight.
- Remove the steak slices from the bowl and reserve the marinade.
- In a wok, heat a little oil and stir fry the steak slices in batches till browned.
- In a small bowl, dissolve the extra corn flour with water.
- In the wok, add all steak slices, reserved marinade, corn flour mixture and stock cube and bring to a boil, stirring continuously.
- Boil till the mixture thickens.
- Serve with the rice.

Servings per Recipe: 4

Timing Information:

Preparation	10 mins
Total Time	20 mins

Nutritional Information:

Calories	550.3
Fat	30.3g
Cholesterol	140.7mg
Sodium	778.6mg
Carbohydrates	26.6g
Protein	40.1g

* Percent Daily Values are based on a 2,000 calorie diet.

Yummy Candies

Ingredients

- 1 C. graham cracker crumbs
- 1 1/2 C. fine coconut
- 1 (6 oz.) packages red Jell-O, any flavour
- 1 (3 oz.) packages red Jell-O, same flavour
- 1 (14 oz.) sweetened condensed milk

Directions

- In a bowl, add the graham crumbs, coconut, large package of jello (dry mix) and milk and mix till well combined.
- Make 1-inch balls from the mixture.
- Roll the balls in remaining package of jello (dry mix).
- Refrigerate to chill before serving.

Servings per Recipe: 1

Timing Information:

Preparation	15 mins
Total Time	35 mins

Nutritional Information:

Calories	860.7
Fat	31.3g
Cholesterol	33.7mg
Sodium	561.9mg
Carbohydrates	135.3g
Protein	16.4g

* Percent Daily Values are based on a 2,000 calorie diet.

Zesty Sorbet With Plums and Orange

Ingredients

- 3/4 lb plum, rinsed, pitted, sliced, and unpeeled
- 1 C. freshly-squeezed orange juice
- 3 tbsp sugar
- 1 tbsp orange zest

Directions

- In a blender, add the plums, orange juice, sugar and orange peel and pulse till smooth.
- Transfer the mixture into a freezer safe dish and freeze for about 4 hours.
- About 30 minutes before serving, puree in the blender and freeze till ready to eat.

Servings per Recipe: 8

Timing Information:

| Preparation | 15 mins |
| Total Time | 4 hrs 15 mins |

Nutritional Information:

Calories	52.5
Fat	0.1g
Cholesterol	0.0mg
Sodium	0.3mg
Carbohydrates	13.0g
Protein	0.5g

* Percent Daily Values are based on a 2,000 calorie diet.

Miami Spritzers

Ingredients

- 5 C. water
- 1 C. fresh blueberries, ripe
- 3 black plums, ripe (pitted and cut into eighths)
- 8 fresh bay leaves, plus extra for garnish
- 1/4 C. sugar, plus
- 2 tbsp sugar
- 8 C. club soda, cold (for serving)

Directions

- In a medium pan, add the water and bring to a boil.
- Add the blueberries, plums, 8 bay leaves and sugar and bring to a boil, covered on high heat.
- Boil for about 20 minutes, stirring occasionally.
- Through a fine sieve, strain the mixture, pressing lightly with a spatula to extract the juice.
- Reserve the bay leaves.

- Return the juice to the pan with the reserved bay leaves on medium heat and simmer for about 10 minutes.
- Discard the bay leaves.
- Remove from the heat and keep aside the syrup to cool.
- For each drink, in a bowl, add 1/4 C. of the plum-blueberry syrup and 1 C. of the cold club soda and gently, beat to mix.
- Transfer into a glass and serve with a garnishing of a bay leaf.

Servings per Recipe: 8

Timing Information:

| Preparation | 8 mins |
| Total Time | 38 mins |

Nutritional Information:

Calories	58.0
Fat	0.1g
Cholesterol	0.0mg
Sodium	52.8mg
Carbohydrates	14.8g
Protein	0.3g

* Percent Daily Values are based on a 2,000 calorie diet.

Enticing Plums

Ingredients

- 3 lbs purple plums
- 1 cinnamon stick
- 2 C. sugar
- 1/4 tsp salt
- 2 C. daiquiri

Directions

- Wash and stem the plums and prick several holes around the stem ends.
- Place the plums in a 2-quart jar.
- Quarter and pit and the plums that will not fit in the jar.
- Then re-pack the jar, interspersing the whole plums with the plum quarters.
- Add the cinnamon stick.
- In a two quart pan, add the sugar, salt and 1 C. of the water and bring to a boil.

- Reduce the heat to low and simmer for about 10 minutes, stirring occasionally.
- Remove from the heat and keep aside the syrup for about 10 minutes to cool.
- Stir in the daiquiri and immediately place the syrup into the jar over the plums, filling the jar up to 1/2-inch from the rim.
- Partly close the jar, leaving a gap for steam to escape and place the jar in the large pan of boiling water for about 10 minutes.
- Carefully remove the jar with a jar lifter and close the lid tightly.
- Cool at room temperature.
- Refrigerate up to 2 weeks.

Servings per Recipe: 1

Timing Information:

Preparation	40 mins
Total Time	40 mins

Nutritional Information:

Calories	1743.3
Fat	1.9g
Cholesterol	0.0mg
Sodium	292.9mg
Carbohydrates	277.7g
Protein	4.7g

* Percent Daily Values are based on a 2,000 calorie diet.

Comforting Beef Dinner

Ingredients

- 1 1/2 kg round beef roast
- 3 tbsp oil
- 45 g French onion soup mix
- 1 C. plum sauce
- 1/4 tsp chili powder
- 1/4 tsp nutmeg
- 1 tsp brown sugar
- 375 ml water
- 2 tsp corn flour (optional)

Directions

- Set your oven to 320 degrees F before doing anything else.
- In a bowl, add the soup mix, sauce, seasonings, sugar and water and mix till well combined.
- Arrange the beef roast in a roasting pan and top with the beer mixture evenly.

- Cover the roasting pan tightly and cook in the oven for about 2 1/2-2 3/4 hours, flipping occasionally.
- Transfer the roast into a platter.
- Place the pan on the stove.
- Add a little corn flour and cook till the pan juices thickens.
- Cut the beef roast in desired slices and serve with the pan sauce.

Servings per Recipe: 5

Timing Information:

| Preparation | 5 mins |
| Total Time | 2 hrs 35 mins |

Nutritional Information:

Calories	616.5
Fat	21.1g
Cholesterol	198.0mg
Sodium	1275.4mg
Carbohydrates	35.6g
Protein	66.5g

* Percent Daily Values are based on a 2,000 calorie diet.

Thai Style Sauce

Ingredients

- 6 C. pitted chopped red plums
- 1 1/2 C. packed brown sugar
- 1 C. sugar
- 1 C. vinegar, 5% acidity
- 1 small onion
- 1 tsp crushed dried chili pepper flakes
- 4 garlic cloves, minced
- 1 tbsp fresh ginger, minced
- 2 tbsp soy sauce
- 1 tbsp Thai basil, minced
- 1 tbsp basil, minced

Directions

- In a large heavy bottom pan, add all the Ingredients and bring to a boil, stirring continuously.
- Cook for about 1 1/2 hours.

- Fill sterilized jars leaving about 1/4-inch from the top.
- Wipe the rims and place lids and rings and process for about 15 minutes.
- Switch off the stove and remove the lid for about 5 minutes.
- Transfer to a towel-lined counter to cool.
- Remove rings and wipe clean, label and place in storage in a cool, and dark place.

Servings per Recipe: 1

Timing Information:

| Preparation | 30 mins |
| Total Time | 2 hrs |

Nutritional Information:

Calories	520.4
Fat	0.6g
Cholesterol	0.0mg
Sodium	423.3mg
Carbohydrates	130.2g
Protein	2.6g

* Percent Daily Values are based on a 2,000 calorie diet.

Swiss Style Cake

Ingredients

PASTRY DOUGH

- 3 C. flour
- 2/3 C. sugar
- 1/2 tsp salt
- 1 tsp baking powder
- 6 oz. butter
- 3 eggs

ALMOND FILLING

- 2 C. blanched almonds
- 2/3 C. sugar
- 1 tsp almond extract
- 6 oz. butter
- 3 large eggs
- 1/2 C. flour
- 2 lbs plums
- 2/3 C. sliced almonds

Directions

- For the dough in a bowl, mix together the flour, sugar, salt and baking powder.
- With a pastry, cutter, cut the butter cut into small pieces and mix till the mixture resembles to fine breadcrumbs.
- Add the eggs and mix till the dough forms a ball.
- Wrap the dough and refrigerate to chill.
- Set your oven to 300 degrees F and grease a flan dish.
- For the almond filling in a food processor, add the almonds and sugar and pulse till finely grind.
- Add the almond extract and butter and mix till smooth.
- Add eggs, one at a time, beating continuously.
- Add the flour and mix well.
- Roll the dough onto a floured surface.
- Arrange the rolled dough into the prepared flan dish and trim the excess edges.
- Place the filling over the dough evenly.
- Remove the stones from plums and slice into quarters.
- Arrange the sliced plums, cut side up over the filling and sprinkle with the sliced almonds evenly.
- Cook in the oven for about 45 minutes.

- Remove from the oven and place onto wire rack to cool completely.
- Serve with a sprinkling of the icing-sugar.

Servings per Recipe: 1

Timing Information:

| Preparation | 20 mins |
| Total Time | 1 hr 5 mins |

Nutritional Information:

Calories	7989.3
Fat	493.9g
Cholesterol	0.0mg
Sodium	423.3mg
Carbohydrates	130.2g
Protein	2.6g

* Percent Daily Values are based on a 2,000 calorie diet.

Lemon Cardamom and Plum Sauce

Ingredients

- 3 lbs plums, seeded, and chopped with skin left on (use food processor)
- 1 C. water
- 1/2 C. lemon lime soda
- 1 lemon, juice of
- 16 cardamom pods, crushed
- 2 tbsp powdered fruit pectin
- 1 tsp vanilla
- 3 1/4 C. sugar

Directions

- Sterilize the jars and lids in the boiling water.
- Line a colander with the cheesecloth and arrange inside a bowl.
- In a large pan, add the plums, water, soda, lemon juice, and cardamom and bring to a boil on high heat.
- Reduce the heat to low and simmer, covered for about 15 minutes.

- Place the plum mixture into colander and drain without pressing the fruit for about 45 minutes.
- Add water to make about 2 3/4 C. of the juice.
- Return juice in the pan with pectin, vanilla and bring to a full boil on high heat.
- Stir in the sugar and bring to a full boil.
- Boil, stirring continuously for about 1 minute.
- Remove from the heat and skim off and discard any foam from top.
- Divide the jelly into hot jars, filling them to within 1/4-inch of their rims.
- Cover each jar with a two-piece lid.
- Place the jars into the canner and process for about 5 minutes, beginning timing when water comes to a boil.
- After 5 minutes, turn off heat and remove canner lid.
- Keep the jars in hot water for about 5 minutes.

Servings per Recipe: 1

Timing Information:

Preparation	0 mins
Total Time	45 mins

Nutritional Information:

Calories	874.7
Fat	1.0g
Cholesterol	0.0mg
Sodium	4.0mg
Carbohydrates	202.8g
Protein	2.5g

* Percent Daily Values are based on a 2,000 calorie diet.

Fresh Salad Armenian Style

Ingredients

- 3 large plums, cut into wedges
- 3 C. spinach, stems removed and leaves torn
- 2 C. cucumbers, pared, seeded and thinly sliced
- 1/4 C. red onion, thinly sliced
- 1/4 C. parsley, minced
- 2 tbsp pistachios, chopped

ARMENIAN DRESSING

- 1/3 C. safflower oil
- 2 -3 tbsp fresh lemon juice
- 1/2 tsp oregano
- 1/2 tsp minced garlic
- 1/4 tsp dry mustard
- pepper

Directions

- In a bowl, mix together the spinach, cucumber, onion, parsley, pistachios and plums.
- In another bowl, add the dressing Ingredients and mix till well combined.
- Place the dressing over the salad and toss to coat well.

Servings per Recipe: 2

Timing Information:

| Preparation | 10 mins |
| Total Time | 13 mins |

Nutritional Information:

Calories	462.3
Fat	40.5g
Cholesterol	0.0mg
Sodium	42.8mg
Carbohydrates	25.3g
Protein	5.0g

* Percent Daily Values are based on a 2,000 calorie diet.

Salmon Asian Style

Ingredients

- 4 -8 oz. salmon fillets
- Asian plum sauce, to taste
- 1/2 C. green onion, chopped

Directions

- Set the broiler of your oven.
- Coat the salmon fillets with the plum sauce evenly.
- In a shallow baking dish, place the salmon fillets and top with half of the green onions.
- Keep aside for about 10 minutes.
- Cook under the broiler for about 10-20 minutes.
- Check after 10 minutes.
- Drizzle with the additional sauce and serve with a sprinkling of the remaining green onions.

Servings per Recipe: 4

Timing Information:

| Preparation | 10 mins |
| Total Time | 25 mins |

Nutritional Information:

Calories	36.5
Fat	0.9g
Cholesterol	0.0mg
Sodium	42.8mg
Carbohydrates	25.3g
Protein	5.0g

* Percent Daily Values are based on a 2,000 calorie diet.

Fruit & Sushi Rice Spring Rolls

Ingredients

- 2 large fresh peaches
- 1 3/4 C. water
- 1 C. short-grain sushi rice
- 3 1/2 tbsps cream of coconut
- 1 pinch salt
- 10 rice paper wrappers
- 1 C. plum preserves
- 2 C. sliced fresh strawberries
- 2 large seedless oranges, peeled and sectioned
- 1 large grapefruit, peeled and sectioned
- 1/4 C. fresh mint leaves, or as desired
- 1 C. vanilla yogurt, or more to taste (optional)

Directions

- In a large pan of boiling water, cook the peaches for about 1 minute and immediately transfer into a bowl of chilled water for several minutes.

- Remove the peaches from the water and, peel, core and cut the peaches into wedges and keep aside.
- In a pan, mix together the rice, water, coconut cream and salt and bring to a boil and reduce the heat to medium-low.
- Simmer, covered for about 20-25 minutes or till the liquid is absorbed
- Remove everything from the heat and keep aside, uncovered to cool completely.
- Soak the wrappers, one by one in a bowl of chilled water till soft and transfer onto a smooth surface.
- In the center of each wrapper, place rice, followed by plum reserves, strawberries, peaches, oranges, grapefruit and mint.
- Roll the wrapper around the filling and with your wet fingers brush the edges and press to seal completely.
- Cut each roll in half and serve with yogurt.

Amount per serving (10 total)

Timing Information:

Preparation	40 m
Cooking	20 m
Total Time	1 h

Nutritional Information:

Calories	267 kcal
Fat	1.7 g
Carbohydrates	60.7g
Protein	3.7 g
Cholesterol	1 mg
Sodium	61 mg

* Percent Daily Values are based on a 2,000 calorie diet.

Jerk Stir-Fry

(Caribbean)

Ingredients

- 1 tbsp vegetable oil
- 1 green bell pepper, seeded and cubed
- 1 red bell pepper, seeded and cubed
- 1/4 cup sliced sweet onions
- 3/4 pound skinless, boneless chicken breast, cut into strips
- 2 1/2 tsps Caribbean jerk seasoning
- 1/2 cup plum sauce
- 1 tbsp soy sauce
- 1/4 cup chopped roasted peanuts

Directions

- Get wok, add oil, and for 7 mins stir fry your onions and peppers until they are soft. Once soft remove them from the pan.
- Get a bowl and combine chicken and jerk seasoning. Evenly coat.
- Stir fry chicken until cooked. Then add plum sauce and onions and peppers. Stir fry for five mins after chicken is cooked.
- Add some soy sauce and peanuts.

- Enjoy.

NOTE: Remember that all stir fries go great with rice.

Servings: 2 servings

Timing Information:

Preparation	Cooking	Total Time
15 mins	20 mins	35 mins

Nutritional Information:

Calories	549 kcal
Carbohydrates	41 g
Cholesterol	104 mg
Fat	21.4 g
Fiber	4.7 g
Protein	44.3 g
Sodium	1621 mg

* Percent Daily Values are based on a 2,000 calorie diet.

Tofu Stir Fry

Ingredients

- 1 (3.5 ounce) package ramen noodles (such as Nissin® Top Ramen)
- 3 tbsps olive oil
- 1 slice firm tofu, cubed
- 1/2 green bell pepper, chopped
- 1/4 small onion, chopped
- 1/3 cup plum sauce
- 1/3 cup sweet and sour sauce

Directions

- Get a pan. Add water and salt. Heat until boiling.
- Use the boiling water to cook your ramen noodles for three mins.
- Get a wok with medium heat get your olive oil hot.
- Fry tofu, onions and pepper for 6 mins.
- The tofu should be on one side of the pan, the onions on another side.
- Combine the ramen with the tofu and peppers.
- Mix in sweet and sour sauce and plum sauce.
- Continue stir frying for three to five mins.

- Let cool and enjoy.

Servings: 2 servings

Timing Information:

Preparation	Cooking	Total Time
10 mins	15 mins	25 mins

Nutritional Information:

Calories	377 kcal
Carbohydrates	35.3 g
Cholesterol	24.2 g
Fat	< 1 mg
Fiber	1.3 g
Protein	3.6 g
Sodium	3.6 g

* Percent Daily Values are based on a 2,000 calorie diet.

Thanks for Reading! Join the Club and Keep on Cooking with 6 More Cookbooks....

http://bit.ly/1TdrStv

To grab the box sets simply follow the link mentioned above, or tap one of book covers.

This will take you to a page where you can simply enter your email address and a PDF version of the box sets will be emailed to you.

Hope you are ready for some serious cooking!

http://bit.ly/1TdrStv

COME ON...
LET'S BE FRIENDS :)

We adore our readers and love connecting with them socially.

Like BookSumo on Facebook and let's get social!

Facebook

And also check out the BookSumo Cooking Blog.

Food Lover Blog

Printed in Great Britain
by Amazon